BECOMING

An exploration of original, hand drawn art
By Angel Cheney

Art is a beautiful medium for relaxation, stress relief, therapy, and pure enjoyment. It is our hope that as you travel through these pages you will be encouraged by what you find and experience. Some of the pages include areas of white space where you can add your own thoughts, dreams, or doodles. Enjoy!

About the artist:

Angel Cheney is an artist, singer/songwriter, poet, and author from the Indianapolis, IN area. She is passionate about taking people on a journey with her through art, words, and music, Check out more of her work at **www.angelcheney.com**

STAY TUNED!
EXCITING NEW BOOKS OF
CONTEMPLATIVE
COLORING
FOR ALL PEOPLE
COMING SOON!

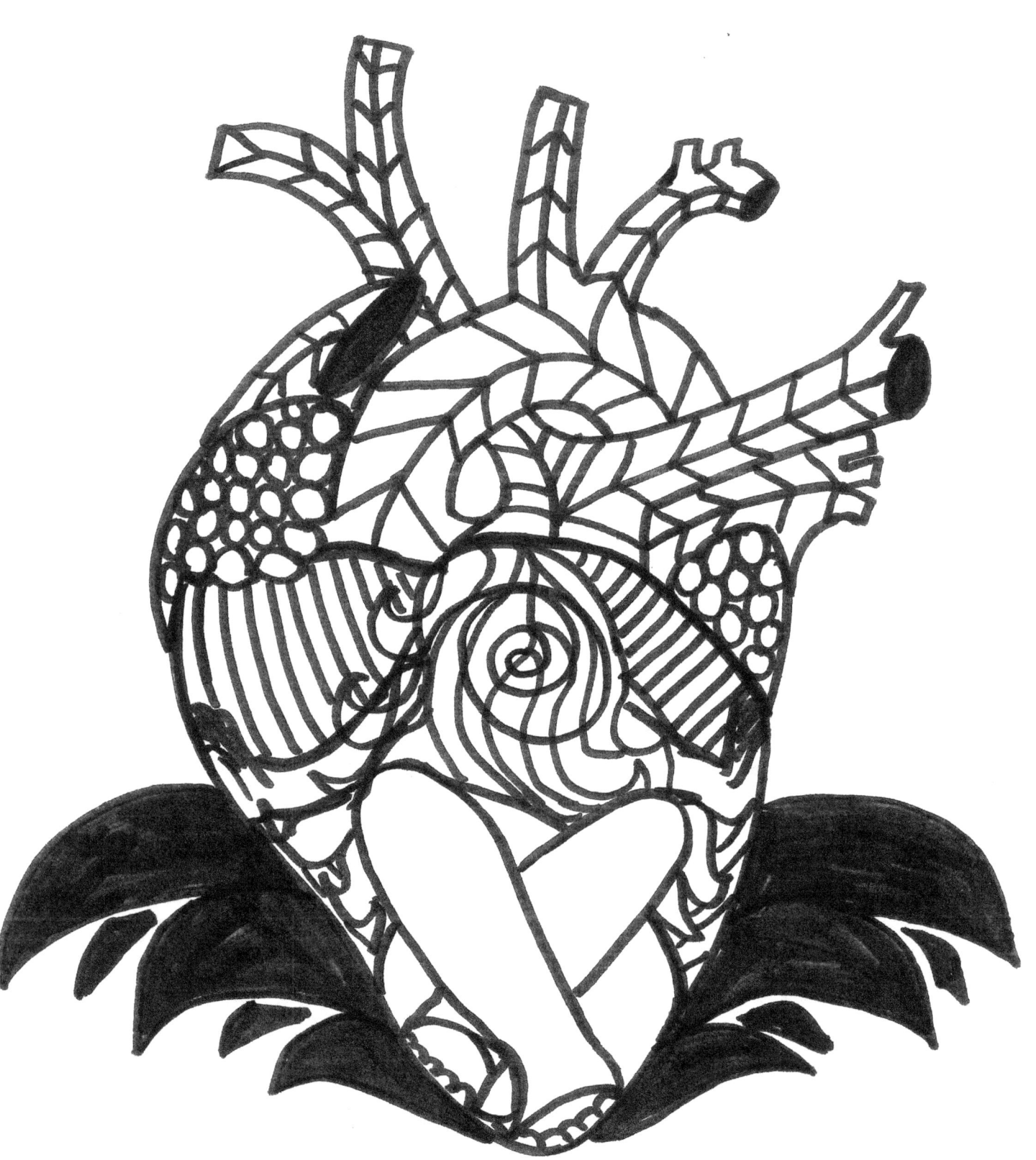

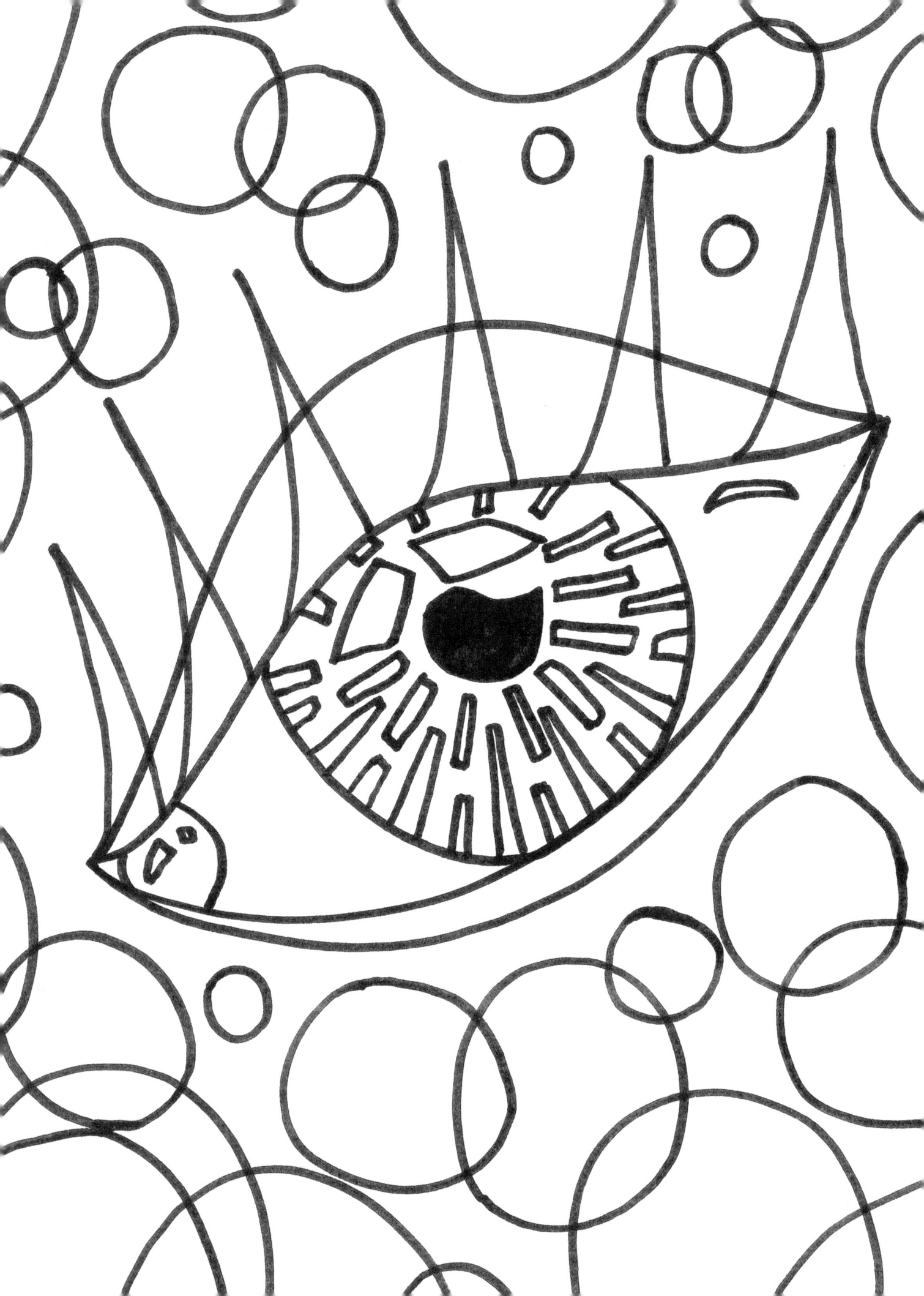

In this life
I have to do
Something
To be
Someone
I
Might
As
Well
Be
Me

I am believing
That the cracking
   acorn
      of my soul
Will grow
      into a powerful
               oak

Trusting
   that each beat of my
      raw
      honest
         heart
is drawing
      me

DEEPER

            into the mystery
      the juxtaposition
   of authenticity and surrender
      where truth reigns
                  and there is peace.

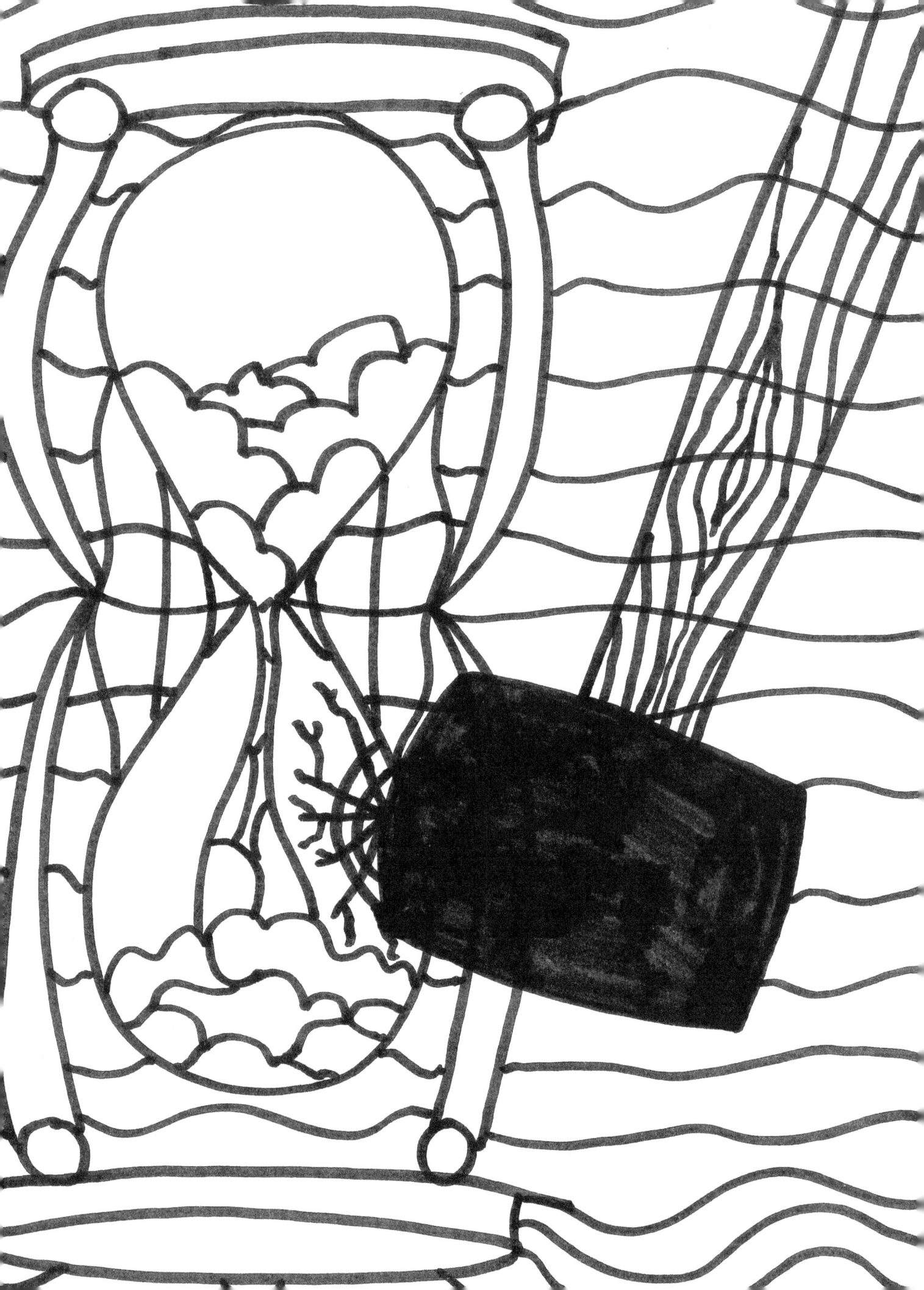

There is a knowing   The essence of God

That whispers

From the center of my existence

That breathes light into the shadowlands

The still darkness of truth

And in that knowing

There

Is

PEACE